STING!

THE SCORPION
AND OTHER ANIMALS THAT STING

Greg Roza

PowerKiDS
press
New York

Published in 2011 by The Rosen Publishing Group, Inc.
29 East 21st Street, New York, NY 10010

First Edition

Editor: Jennifer Way
Book Design: Kate Laczynski

Photo Credits: Cover, pp. 1, 17 Shutterstock.com; p. 4 Tim Flach/Getty Images; p. 5 Hemera/Thinkstock; p. 6 Jupiterimages/Photos.com/Thinkstock; p. 7 (top) © www.iStockphoto.com/Marissa Childs; p. 7 (bottom) © www.iStockphoto.com/Borut Trdina; p. 8 Franz Aberham/Getty Images; p. 9 © Christophe Véchot/Peter Arnold, Inc.; p. 10 © www.iStockphoto.com/Ameng Wu; p. 11 © www.iStockphoto.com/Pgiam; p. 12 John & Barbara Gerlach/Getty Images; p. 13 Imagemore Co, Ltd./Getty Images; p. 14 Dr. David Phillips/Getty Images; pp. 15 (left, right), 19 (top) iStockphoto/Thinkstock; p. 16 James H. Robinson/Getty Images; p. 18 Justin Sullivan/Getty Images; pp. 20–21 Claus Meyer/Getty Images; p. 22 Paulo De Oliveira/Getty Images.

Library of Congress Cataloging-in-Publication Data

Roza, Greg.
 Sting! : the scorpion and other animals that sting / by Greg Roza. — 1st ed.
    p. cm. — (Armed and dangerous)
 Includes index.
 ISBN 978-1-4488-2548-6 (library binding) — ISBN 978-1-4488-2680-3 (pbk.) —
 ISBN 978-1-4488-2681-0 (6-pack)
 1. Scorpions—Juvenile literature. 2. Bees—Juvenile literature. 3. Bites and stings—
Juvenile literature. I. Title.
 QL458.7.R69 2011
 591.47—dc22

                                          2010023604

Manufactured in the United States of America

CPSIA Compliance Information: Batch #WW11PK: For Further Information contact Rosen Publishing, New York, New York at 1-800-237-9932

CONTENTS

On the Attack! 4

How Stingers Work 6

Predator and Prey...8

Scorpions and Their Stingers 10

Scorpion Venom.. 12

Honeybees 14

Wasps... 16

Stingrays 18

Fun Facts 20

Don't Get Stung!.. 22

Glossary 23

Index... 24

Web Sites 24

Scorpions use their front claws to hold on to prey while giving it a sting.

Animals have many ways of staying safe in the wild. Some animals have hard shells. Some have colors that allow them to hide in plain sight. Others run very fast. Some animals have a painful sting!

Have you ever been stung by a bee? If so, then you know that its stinger is an effective

A bee's sharp stinger is at the end of its body. Bees sting to defend themselves, rather than to hunt.

weapon! Animals with stingers, such as scorpions, bees, and wasps, use them to scare off **predators**. Some animals use them to shoot **venom** into their **prey**. Venom can stun or even kill an animal, allowing the stinging animal to eat its prey.

HOW STINGERS WORK

All stingers work in the same basic way. A stinger's tip has a sharp point like a needle. The point allows the stinger to **pierce** the skin or hide of an animal. However, not all stingers are exactly the same. Some

Stingrays have venomous tail spines that they use to defend themselves. Shown here is a blue-spotted ribbontail ray.

stingers have tiny **barbs** on them. The barbs make the stinger stick firmly inside the animal.

Some animals have hollow stingers so they can shoot venom into the animal's body. Venom can cause pain and itching. It can also stun or kill. For example, all scorpions have venom. However, only some scorpions are deadly to people.

PREDATOR AND PREY

Some predators use their stingers to hunt. However, it is often their venom that kills prey, not the sting itself. Venom enters the prey's bloodstream when the stinger pierces its skin. Different venoms work in different ways. For example, some venoms stop the heart from beating. Some stop the lungs from breathing. Others **paralyze** an animal.

The venom in a scorpion's sting paralyzes its prey so that the scorpion can eat it.

Other animals use stingers to defend themselves from predators. Animals often stay away from animals with stingers because they know it hurts to be stung! Many scorpions use their stingers both to hunt and to chase away predators.

SCORPIONS AND THEIR STINGERS

Scorpions are **arachnids** that live mostly in hot, dry places. They can be found in grasslands, deserts, forests, caves, and on seashores. Scorpions have eight legs and two big claws. All scorpions have stingers on the ends of their tails. They use their stingers to chase away predators and also to hunt prey.

Here is a close-up view of a scorpion's stinger. Of the 1,400 kinds of scorpions, only about 25 have venom that is dangerous to people.

Many kinds of scorpions live in deserts, like Valley of the Gods in Utah, shown here.

Scorpions hide under rocks or plants. When an unlucky bug or small animal wanders by, the scorpion strikes! The scorpion uses its claws and legs to grab the prey. Then it quickly stings the prey. The scorpion's stinger shoots venom into the animal.

SCORPION VENOM

Some scorpion venoms are weak, and other scorpion venoms are strong. Many types of scorpion venom are strong enough to paralyze or kill most bugs. Some venoms are strong enough to kill small animals, such as mice and frogs. Once the venom starts to work, the scorpion eats its prey.

Some scorpion venoms are powerful enough to paralyze or kill small animals, such as this mouse.

Most scorpion stings are painful and can make a person sick. However, only about 25 scorpions in the world have venom strong enough to kill people. The scorpion with the strongest venom is called the deathstalker. It lives in northern Africa and the Middle East.

HONEYBEES

When talking about animals that sting, most people think of honeybees. Honeybees do not use their stingers to hunt. They use them to defend themselves and their hives. Honeybee stingers have barbs on them. The stingers have weak venom, which in most people

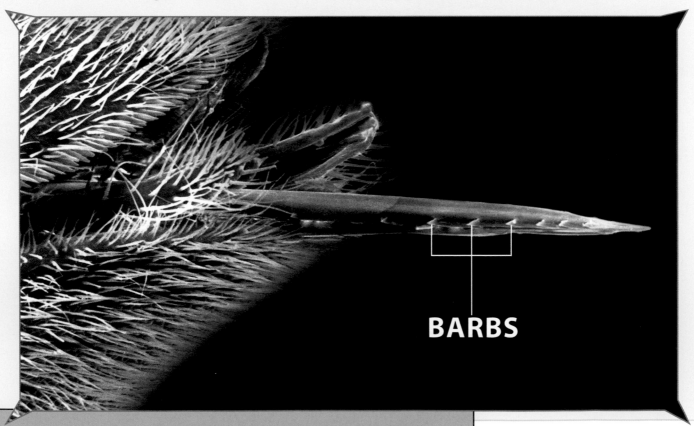

BARBS

This is a close-up of a bee's stinger. You can see the barbs that help the stinger stick in an animal's skin.

Honeybees build honeycombs in their hives. Honeycombs are made to store honey. Honeycombs also hold young bees, which are called larvae.

causes pain, swelling, and itching. However, receiving numerous honeybee stings at one time can cause illness and even death.

When a honeybee stings, the barbs on its stinger hold tight in the animal's skin. The stinger often remains behind when the bee flies away. The venom continues to enter the animal's body. The honeybee dies soon after.

Honeybees gather pollen and nectar from flowers. Nectar is the stuff that honeybees turn into honey.

WASPS

Wasps are closely related to bees. Some kinds of wasps even look like bees. Wasp stingers have barbs, too. However, a wasp's stinger is smaller than a bee's stinger. This allows the wasp to keep its stinger after stinging an animal.

Wasps use their stingers both for hunting and scaring away enemies. Wasp venom paralyzes small prey. Once the prey stops

This wasp used its stinger to paralyze this caterpillar. The caterpillar will be used to feed wasp larvae in the hive.

In this close-up of a wasp's nest, you can see the wasp larvae that fill some of the nest's cells.

moving, the wasp takes it back to its hive. The prey is used to feed young wasps. When a wasp stings a person, the venom causes pain and itching. Many wasp stings at one time can be more dangerous.

STINGRAYS

Scorpions and bees are not the only animals that have stingers. Stingrays are wide, flat fish that live in oceans around the world. They have long tails with sharp, barbed stingers on the ends. Stingrays use their stingers to scare away enemies, not for hunting.

Stingrays generally do not attack people. They often lie on the seabed in **shallow**

Stingray stings can be deadly. Steve Irwin, shown here, hosted TV shows about animals. He died from a stingray sting in 2006.

Stingrays generally stay close to the ocean floor. This can make them hard for people to see when swimming. Most people who are stung by a stingray do not die from the sting or its venom.

water. Their shape and coloring make them hard to see. People walking and swimming can get stung when they scare resting stingrays. Stingray venom causes pain, but it is generally not strong enough to kill a person.

FUN FACTS

1 Female scorpions can have 25 to 35 babies at one time.

2 Baby scorpions ride on their mothers' backs until they are old enough to take care of themselves.

3 Most scorpions live alone. They sometimes sting and eat other scorpions that wander into their territory.

Only female wasps and bees have stingers.

Some wasps use their stingers to lay eggs on or inside their prey. When the eggs hatch, the baby wasps eat the prey!

Stingray venom does not often kill people. However, a sting to the heart or belly can cause enough bleeding to kill.

DON'T GET STUNG!

Most scorpions in the United States are not dangerous. Some people even keep scorpions as pets! Scorpions generally stay away from people, but they will attack if someone gets too close. Only one type of scorpion in the United States, the bark scorpion, has venom strong enough to kill a person.

Scorpion, bee, and wasp stings cause pain, itching, and swelling. Some people, however, are **allergic** to insect stings. For these people, one bee sting can be deadly. They must be prepared to take a drug if they are ever stung.

GLOSSARY

allergic (uh-LER-jik) Getting a little sick from something.

arachnids (uh-RAK-nidz) Types of animals, such as scorpions, spiders, and ticks.

barbs (BARBZ) Sharp spikes with hooks at the ends.

paralyze (PER-uh-lyz) To cause an animal to lose feeling or movement.

pierce (PIRS) To make a hole in something.

predators (PREH-duh-terz) Animals that kill other animals for food.

prey (PRAY) An animal that is hunted by another animal for food.

shallow (SHA-low) Not deep.

venom (VEH-num) A poison passed by one animal into another through a bite or a sting.

INDEX

B
barbs, 7, 14–16
bee(s), 4–5, 15–16,
    18, 21–22
body, 7, 15

C
claws, 10–11

H
heart, 8, 21
hide, 6

I
itching, 7, 15, 17, 22

L
legs, 10–11
lungs, 8

N
needle, 6

P
pain, 7, 15, 17, 19, 22
people, 7, 13–14,
    17–19, 21–22
point, 6
predators, 5, 8–10
prey, 5, 8, 10–12,
    16–17, 21

S
shells, 4
skin, 6, 8, 15
stinger(s), 4, 5–11,
    14–16, 18, 21

T
tails, 10, 18

V
venom(s), 5, 7–8,
    11–17, 19, 21–22

W
wasp(s), 5, 16–17, 21–22

WEB SITES

Due to the changing nature of Internet links, PowerKids Press has
developed an online list of Web sites related to the subject of this
book. This site is updated regularly. Please use this link to access
the list:
www.powerkidslinks.com/armd/sting/